Sarah Morgan Bryan Platt

A Woman's Poems

Sarah Morgan Bryan Platt

A Woman's Poems

ISBN/EAN: 9783744717809

Printed in Europe, USA, Canada, Australia, Japan

Cover: Foto ©Thomas Meinert / pixelio.de

More available books at **www.hansebooks.com**

A WOMAN'S POEMS.

BOSTON:
JAMES R. OSGOOD AND COMPANY,
LATE TICKNOR & FIELDS, AND FIELDS, OSGOOD & CO.
1871

Entered according to act of Congress, in the year 1871, by

MRS. S. M. B. PIATT,

In the office of the Librarian of Congress, at Washington, D. C.

PRESS OF R. W. CARROLL & CO.,
CINCINNATI, O.

CONTENTS.

	PAGE
To my Nearest Neighbor,	iii
The Fancy Ball,	1
After Wings,	3
Her Metaphors,	4
The Little Stockings,	6
Lion or Lamb,	8
Twelve Hours Apart,	9
To-Day,	11
My Babes in the Wood,	13
My Ghost,	15
Shapes of a Soul,	18
Death before Death,	20
Meeting a Mirror,	23
The Brother's Hand,	25
The Highest Mountain,	45
Offers for the Child,	46
Her Last Gift,	48
A Sister of Mercy.	50
Earth in Heaven,	52
Last Words,	54
My Artist,	56
In the Graveyard,	59
The End of the Rainbow,	62
Two Blush-Roses,	64
Of a Parting,	66

CONTENTS.

	PAGE
A Child's First Sight of Snow,	68
A Lily of the Nile,	69
A Disenchantment,	71
The Flowers in the Ground,	73
Questions of the Hour,	74
Gaslight and Starlight,	76
A Dream's Awakening,	78
Talk about Ghosts,	79
A Year—MDCCCLX,	81
On a Wedding Day,	88
The Dove and the Angel,	90
Her Talk with a Redbird,	92
My Wedding Ring,	93
A Falling Star,	94
Playing Beggars,	96
Stone for a Statue,	99
A Bird's Wing and a Soul's,	100
Fallen Angels,	102
To Marian Asleep,	103
A President at Home,	105
An Eagle's Plume from Palestine,	107
A Chain from Venice,	109
A Walk to My Own Grave,	110
Paris,	113
An After Poem,	114

WITH DISTANT ECHOES.

	PAGE
Hearing the Battle,	117
The Christmas Tree Out-of-Doors,	119
A Night and Morning,	121
Army of Occupation,	123
April at Washington,	125
—— to ——,	127

TO

MY NEAREST NEIGHBOR.

LOVED AS MYSELF—AND MORE!

THIS BOOK IS YOURS, NOT MINE, TO GIVE OR TAKE.

YOUR HAND, NOT MINE, HAS SENT IT FROM YOUR DOOR.

MY HEART GOES WITH IT—ONLY FOR YOUR SAKE.

WASHINGTON, D. C.

A WOMAN'S POEMS.

THE FANCY BALL.

As Morning you'd have me rise
   On that shining world of art;
You forget: I have too much dark in my eyes—
   And too much dark in my heart.

"Then go as the Night—in June:
   Pass, dreamily, by the crowd,
With jewels to mock the stars and the moon,
   And shadowy robes like cloud.

"Or as Spring, with a spray in your hair
   Of blossoms as yet unblown;
It will suit you well, for our youth should wear
   The bloom in the bud alone.

"Or drift from the outer gloom
  With the soft white silence of Snow:"
I should melt myself with the warm, close room—
  Or my own life's burning. No.

"Then fly through the glitter and mirth
  As a Bird of Paradise:"
Nay, the waters I drink have touch'd the earth:
  I breathe no summer of spice.

"Then —" Hush: if I go at all,
  (It will make them stare and shrink,
It will look so strange at a Fancy Ball,)
  I will go as — Myself, I think!

AFTER WINGS.

This was your butterfly, you see.
   His fine wings made him vain?—
The caterpillars crawl, but he
   Pass'd them in rich disdain?—
My pretty boy says, "Let him be
   Only a worm again?"

Oh, child, when things have learn'd to wear
   Wings once, they must be fain
To keep them always high and fair.
   Think of the creeping pain
Which even a butterfly must bear
   To be a worm again!

HER METAPHORS.

A FAIRY dream that stole,
  With evanescent light,
Across thy waken'd soul,
  One early Autumn night—
      Am I not this to thee?

A lone and languid rose
  That in thy care might bloom,
But on the distance throws,
  Vainly, its vague perfume—
      Am I not this to thee?

A faint and trembling star
  That drew thine eyes awhile,
Still shining on afar,
  Deserted by thy smile—
      Am I not this to thee?

HER METAPHORS.

A pearl cast at thy feet
  And worn by thee an hour,
Then left where fierce waves beat,
  The plaything of their power—
    Am I not this to thee?

A half-remember'd strain,
  That once could charm thine ear,
Whose music thou again
  Wilt sometimes sigh to hear—
    Am I not this to thee?

THE LITTLE STOCKINGS.

(ON CHRISTMAS EVE.)

He will see sweet Stockings, cunning and new,
    Warm in scarlet, and dainty in white—
Stockings that never have crept in a shoe—
    Waiting his morning's enchanted light.

And other glad Stockings, that he should know—
    Grown larger, perhaps, than they were last year!—
In many a pretty, half-sleepy row
    They wonder, no doubt, if he is near!

This Saint of the children, who loves them so,
    Fairily filling each color'd space,
Will touch clear dreams with his kiss—and go
    With tears, I think, in his tender face.

Ah, spite of his furs, he will shiver, I fear,
    At the thought of some Stockings, bright and small,
Whose curious looks are no longer here,
    Awake for him, by the lonesome wall!

THE LITTLE STOCKINGS.

Oh, you whose little hands reach no more
  Toward his gray, kind beard in their dimpled play,
Whose little feet pass'd through the great, dim Door,
  With never a step nor a sound, away:

Have you found Another, who lights with love
  His Birthday Tree for your charmèd eyes?
Do you see in its branches the snow-white Dove?
  Is it fair with the flowering fruit of the skies?

LION OR LAMB?

Which of the Two shall be victor at last,
   After this desperate battle is done?
Temper the wind, for the shorn strength fails fast.
   Look how the yellow Life shakes with the sun
It has fed on afar in wastes of its own!
   Then the cruel wild glitter of sand
   Looks hot in its eye! Shall I stand,
And watch them, and leave them alone?

Let them fight on, as they will and they must—
   Yet somehow the one is so pretty and white!
Say, dainty wool, must the blood and the dust
   Hide your soft snowiness all from my sight?
Ah—wait? I *have* waited so long——
   The roar of the desert, it dies;
   A timid bleat goes to the skies:
The Lamb of the Two is the strong!

TWELVE HOURS APART.

He loved me.   But he loved, likewise,
  This morning's world in bloom and wings;
Ah, does he love the world that lies
  In dampness, whispering shadowy things,
    Under this little band of moon?

He loves me?   Will he fail to see
  A phantom hand has touch'd my hair
(And waver'd, withering, over me)
  To leave a subtle grayness there,
    Below the outer shine of June?

He loves me?   Would he call it fair,
  The flush'd half-flower he left me, say?
For it has pass'd beneath the glare
  And from my bosom drops away,
    Shaken into the grass with pain?

TWELVE HOURS APART.

He loves me? Well, I do not know.
  A song in plumage cross'd the hill
At sunrise when I felt him go—
  And song and plumage now are still.
    He could not praise the bird again.

He loves me? Vail'd in mist I stand,
  My veins less high with life than when
To-day's thin dew was in the land,
  Vaguely less beautiful than then—
    Myself a dimness with the dim.

He loves me? I am faint with fear.
  He never saw me quite so old;
I never met him quite so near
  My grave, nor quite so pale and cold:
    ——Nor quite so sweet, he says, to him!

TO-DAY.

Ah, real thing of bloom and breath,
  I can not love you while you stay.
Put on the dim, still charm of death,
  Fade to a phantom, float away,
  And let me call you Yesterday!

Let empty flower-dust at my feet
  Remind me of the buds you wear;
Let the bird's quiet show how sweet
  The far-off singing made the air;
  And let your dew through frost look fair.

In mourning you I shall rejoice.
  Go: for the bitter word may be
A music—in the vanish'd voice;
  And on the dead face I may see
  How bright its frown has been to me.

TO-DAY.

Then in the haunted grass I'll sit,
   Half tearful in your wither'd place,
And watch your lovely shadow flit
   Across To-morrow's sunny face,
     And vex her with your perfect grace.

So, real thing of bloom and breath,
   I weary of you while you stay.
Put on the dim, still charm of death,
   Fade to a phantom, float away,
     And let me call you Yesterday!

MY BABES IN THE WOOD.

I know a story, fairer, dimmer, sadder,
   Than any story painted in your books.
You are so glad? It will not make you gladder;
   Yet listen, with your pretty restless looks.

"Is it a Fairy Story?" Well, half fairy—
   At least it dates far back as fairies do,
And seems to me as beautiful and airy;
   Yet half, perhaps the fairy half, is true.

You had a baby sister and a brother,
   (Two very dainty people, rosily white,
Each sweeter than all things except the other!)
   Older yet younger—gone from human sight!

And I, who loved them, and shall love them ever,
   And think with yearning tears how each light hand
Crept toward bright bloom or berries—I shall never
   Know how I lost them. Do you understand?

MY BABES IN THE WOOD.

Poor slightly golden heads! I think I miss'd them
   First, in some dreamy, piteous, doubtful way;
But when and where with lingering lips I kiss'd them,
   My gradual parting, I can never say.

Sometimes I fancy that they may have perish'd
   In shadowy quiet of wet rocks and moss,
Near paths whose very pebbles I have cherish'd,
   For their small sakes, since my most lovely loss.

I fancy, too, that they were softly cover'd
   By robins, out of apple-flowers they knew,
Whose nursing wings in far home sunshine hover'd,
   Before the timid world had dropp'd the dew.

Their names were—what yours are! At this you wonder.
   Their pictures are—your own, as you have seen;
And my bird-buried darlings, hidden under
   Lost leaves—why, it is your dead selves I mean!

MY GHOST.

A STORY TOLD TO MY LITTLE COUSIN KATE.

YES, Katie, I think you are very sweet,
   Now that the tangles are out of your hair,
And you sing as well as the birds you meet,
   That are playing, like you, in the blossoms there.
But now you are coming to kiss me, you say:
   Well, what is it for? Shall I tie your shoe,
Or loop your sleeve in a prettier way?
   "Do I know about ghosts?" Indeed I do.

"Have I seen one?" Yes: last evening, you
     know,
   We were taking a walk that you had to miss,
(I think you were naughty and cried to go,
   But, surely, you'll stay at home after this!)
And, away in the twilight lonesomely
   ("What is the twilight?" It's—getting late!)
I was thinking of things that were sad to me—
   There, hush! you know nothing about them,
     Kate.

MY GHOST.

Well, we had to go through the rocky lane,
   Close to that bridge where the water roars,
By a still, red house, where the dark and rain
   Go in when they will at the open doors;
And the moon, that had just waked up, look'd through
   The broken old windows and seem'd afraid,
And the wild bats flew and the thistles grew
   Where once in the roses the children play'd.

Just across the road by the cherry-trees
   Some fallen white stones had been lying so long,
Half hid in the grass, and under these
   There were people dead. I could hear the song
Of a very sleepy dove, as I pass'd
   The graveyard near, and the cricket that cried;
And I look'd (ah! the Ghost is coming at last!)
   And something was walking at my side.

It seem'd to be wrapp'd in a great dark shawl,
   (For the night was a little cold, you know.)
It would not speak. It was black and tall;
   And it walk'd so proudly and very slow.
Then it mock'd me—every thing I could do:
   Now it caught at the lightning-flies like me;
Now it stopp'd where the elder-blossoms grew;
   Now it tore the thorns from a gray bent tree.

Still it follow'd me under the yellow moon,
    Looking back to the graveyard now and then,
Where the winds were playing the night a tune—
    But, Kate, a Ghost does n't care for *men*,
And your papa *couldn't* have done it harm!
    Ah, dark-eyed darling, what is it you see?
There, you needn't hide in your dimpled arm—
    It was only my Shadow that walk'd with me!

SHAPES OF A SOUL.

White with the starlight folded in its wings,
   And nestling timidly against your love,
At this soft time of hush'd and glimmering things,
   You call my soul a dove, a snowy dove.

If I shall ask you in some shining hour,
   When bees and odors through the clear air pass,
You'll say my soul buds as a small flush'd flower,
   Far off, half-hiding, in the old home-grass.

Ah, pretty names for pretty moods; and you,
   Who love me, such sweet shapes as these can see;
But, take it from its sphere of bloom and dew,
   And where will then your bird or blossom be?

Could you but see it, by life's torrid light,
   Crouch in its sands and glare with fire-red wrath,
My soul would seem a tiger, fierce and bright
   Among the trembling passions in its path.

SHAPES OF A SOUL.

And, could you sometimes watch it coil and slide,
   And drag its colors through the dust a while,
And hiss its poison under-foot, and hide,
   My soul would seem a snake——Ah, do not smile!

Yet fiercer forms and darker it can wear;
   No matter, though, when these are of the Past,
If as a lamb in the Good Shepherd's care
   By the still waters it lie down at last.

DEATH BEFORE DEATH.

ARE mine the empty eyes
That stare toward the little new grave on the beautiful
    burial-hill?
Was mine the last wet kiss that lies
Shut up in his coffin, kissing him still,
          Kissing him still?

Is mine the hollow room?
Was it not cruel to take all the pretty small furniture,
    say?—
The fairy pictures and heaps of bloom,
And music of mock-harps—so far away,
          So far away?

Is mine the hidden face
That one night's sudden dread watching has thinn'd
    and faded so much?—
Mine the lonesome hands through bitter space,
Yearning for something they never can touch,
          Never can touch?

DEATH BEFORE DEATH.

  Is mine the passionate pain
That will hearken the trembling wind and feel the wide
   still snow,
  And sob at night with the sobbing rain,
And only feel that I can not know,
    I can not know?

  Was mine that lovely child?
Did he drop from my heart and go where the Powers
   of the Dust can destroy?
  Can I see the very way he smiled——
" Let God keep his angels"? Do I want my boy—
   I want my boy?

  Is he gone from his air,
From his sun, from his voice, his motion, his mother,
   his world, and his skies,
  From the unshorn light in his sweet hair,
From the elusion of his butterflies,
   His butterflies?

  If not, why let me go
Where another sorrow is watching a small, cold bed
   alone,
  And whisper how I have loved her so,

DEATH BEFORE DEATH.

That to save her darling I gave my own,
   I gave my own!

  Ah! if I learn'd her part,
And my dark fancies but play'd in despair like tragedy
   queens,
 Then my only audience was my heart,
And my tears, that *were* tears, were behind the scenes,
   Behind the scenes.

MEETING A MIRROR.

BELOVED of beautiful and eager eyes,
   It had its honors from the guests below;
But it went somewhat nearer to the skies
   As it grew old, you know.

Still, from the gilded splendor of the day
   That Vanity sees shining in its place,
I turn'd with yearning for the pleased, slow way
   It used to hold my face.

Far up the stair and shunn'd of faded eyes
   I found the thing that I had loved before:
It took my face, grew dead-white with surprise,
   Held it—then saw no more!

Suddenly blinded: for the Mirror shed
   Tears for dim hair, it praised to suns gone by,
And One to whom once of it I gayly said,
   "My rival—dear as I!"

MEETING A MIRROR.

Companions, in our time, of pleasant lights,
   I thought, and music and rich foreign blooms,
What shall we find for those fair evening-sights
   In lonesome upper rooms?

The misty Mirror show'd a calm reproof,
   Receiving there a higher company,
In dust and empty silence near the roof,
   Than we were wont to see.

Its pride in jewel'd reverence was gone,
   And quiet tenderness was in its place,
That took the sweet stars, as they glimmer'd on
   In chill clouds, to its grace.

THE BROTHER'S HAND.

Lost somewhere in the wilds of Mexico,
   A poor dry mountain crouches in the sand.
About it, goldenly, the Summers go
   And feed with fruit the gorgeous-colored land,
Yet leave it starving on its empty plain,
Forgotten almost by the tender rain,
   With loneliness around it like a band.

Nor wing'd nor odorous life glows in the air,
   That, dull and dying, toward it heavily creeps,
Yet on its breast, among the clouds, how fair
   A strange calm Image sleeps—and sleeps and
      sleeps!
It is a Man, gigantic, gray in stone,
With dropping eyelids, lying there alone
   With the old awful silence that he keeps.

THE BROTHER'S HAND.

Sharp Southern lightnings on his rocky height
   Against him in their glittering fury fall;
The desert's dumbness smites him day and night;
   Suns scorch him—but he does not stir at all.
Ages, like bubbles, on his slumber break:—
But glimmering legends say he will awake,
   And simple hearts are listening for his call.

For once he was that fabled king, they say,
   Whose savage splendor, wavering from the dark
Of long tradition, seems a dream to-day,
   Yet still the traveler sometimes stops to mark
In solitary places, shining slow,
(Ah, beautiful belief in long ago!)
   The faithful fire in many a tremulous spark.

The languid Spaniard rose and sank again.
   Ardent and light-heroic over seas
The young fair Austrian alien drifted then,
   And made him a mock throne and tried to please
Himself with playing—till his play was doom'd
And through the world his echoing death-shot boom'd.
   The sleeping monarch hears not sounds like these.

He waits. And waiting bosoms know, at last
   Those faithful fires they keep will charm him down

THE BROTHER'S HAND.

Into the jewel'd glory of his Past,
  To beat the dust from off his buried crown,
And trail the brightness of his risen name
Across the risen kingdom he shall claim,
  Though at his coming newer kings may frown.

So there are lives about us, every-where,
  Fruit-fed by tropic suns, yet poison creeps
Across one mountain held by desert air,
  Whereon one Image sleeps — and sleeps and
    sleeps!
It is a Man, gigantic, gray in stone,
With dropping eyelids, lying there alone
  With the old awful silence that he keeps.

And if one stranger waste their wealth awhile,
  And if another act a tragedy
And close the last scene with a desperate smile:
  The sovereign sleeper may not wake to see;
The image on the mountain may not hear
The play-king's death-shot, though it hisses near,
  Or cries afar for many an echoing mile.

He waits. And waiting bosoms know at last
  The faithful fires they keep will charm him down

THE BROTHER'S HAND.

Into the jewel'd glory of his Past,
  To beat the dust from off his buried crown,
And trail the brightness of his risen name
Across the risen kingdom he shall claim,
  Though at his coming newer kings may frown.

———

Here, see what I have brought you from the hill—
  A brier-rose lingering late into July.
Oh, it may tell you, if it can and will,
  In its small way, so pink and timid, why
It waited after all its mates were dead,
And wore for mourning-garments only red
  While its step-mother month was fierce and dry.

There is no flower with look and bloom and breath,
  I faintly fancy, like the faint brier-rose;
No flower so fair for life, so sweet for death,
  That in the dew or in the darkness grows;
No flower that has so fairily heard and seen
What fairy things the hum and honey mean,
  When in the wind the bee about it blows.

Far off, by black-gray stone, in shatter'd heaps,
  The beautiful, familiar, sad home-grace,

THE BROTHER'S HAND.

Like love itself made palpable, it keeps
   Through all the sorrowful forsaken place.
Nor can you find the scented presence there,
On the green ground or in the pensive air,
   Of any other of the blossoming race.

A very lovely woman loved to wear
   Its cluster of blushes once upon her breast.
She brought it from the woods and set it where
   She always loved to be, herself, the best.
The very flowers we think so frail outstay
Our frailer selves—and she is gone away:
   Away—and, therefore, as we think, to rest.

On the seventh birthday of her fair twin-boys,
   She gave the two a boat, as they were one,
(For until then each own'd the other's toys;)
   But when they saw it floating in the sun,
With sails of stained silk so prettily blown,
Each felt that he was now himself alone:
   The golden chain that bound them was undone.

"No, it is mine," each to the other said,
   And one raised up an angry arm and made

THE BROTHER'S HAND.

A quick wide wound, that look'd so strange and red
   Each of the other dimly felt afraid.
Then a child-Cain in shadowy terror stood,
And, crying from the ground, his brother's blood
   Rose from the pleasant shore where they had play'd.

That sharp, swift cut had cleft the two apart.
   And, under his light, lovely hair, one wore
A strange-shaped scar. And in the other's heart,
   A heart that had been very sweet before,
The snake-like passions started from their sleep
And over it began to writhe and creep.
   And so the two were two forevermore.

As they grew older, he who wore the scar
   Saw it was like a hand—his brother's hand,
It seem'd, against him. Then he went afar
   With a kind kinsman to a colder land,
After he heard the dust begin to fall
On his young mother's coffin. She was all
   He had dear. And she was what the shadows are.

Blue-eyed and stately, with a bright, brave scorn
   Of wrong, he in a calmer climate grew.

THE BROTHER'S HAND.

The other, tropic-nursed as tropic-born,
  Was fierce and swarthy, and imperious too,
And restless as the wind that bloweth where
It listeth : so he wander'd here and there.
  And neither of the other clearly knew.

At last there came a heavy hail of lead
  Out of the Northern sky, that Southward fell.
The fields were blasted and the men lay dead ;
  The women moan'd ; and flying shapes of shell
Their ways from roof to hearth-stone madly tore,
And open'd suddenly the deserted door,
  By the brier-roses guarded once so well.

And Ruin glided up the weedy path,
  And cross'd the moldy threshold and went in,
And sat there, with a sort of a sullen wrath,
  Gathering about her all that once had been
Dear and familiar—save the rose, beside
The crumbling porch, from which she vainly tried,
  Tearing her hands with thorns, the flowers to win.

And once, when a great ghastly Sight close by
  Was terrible in the stillness of the moon,

THE BROTHER'S HAND.

A tall, slight soldier, with a smother'd cry,
   Crept close and broke some buds and vanish'd soon;
But, with an almost human joy-in-grief,
The desolate rose-tree thrill'd from root to leaf
   When he said wearily: " Yes—it is I."

A whole year more, when summer flush'd again,
   Near to the same place, in the glitter of heat,
(The earth was red, the sky was smoky then,)
   One lay in agony. Against his feet
A gash'd and gory flag from its shot staff
Flutter'd and fell. There was a cruel laugh
   From one he had not fear'd again to meet;

And a swift horse, deep-black, with foaming mouth
   And angry eyes full of wild wonder, sprung
From its light rider—one who loved the South
   With his whole bitter soul. And, as he flung
The reins away and stood in tears beside
The dying creature, gentle, till it died,
   He show'd that he was desperate, dark, and young.

There was a beautiful and dreadful charm
   About that youthful captain, as he stood

THE BROTHER'S HAND.

Bare-headed, swordless, with his dead right arm
   Loose at his side, his left, whose strength was good,
About his horse—forgetting his own wound,
Forgetting all the horrible things around—
   Calling it all the tender names he could.

But when his horse was gone, he turn'd away
   And stamp'd the fallen flag and cursed, and shook
The tall, slight soldier in whose blood it lay,
   Till he half-raised himself with a dim look,
That made the other loose his hateful hold
And tremble for an instant and grow cold,
   As if his thought some deadly trouble took.

Then he crept closer to the wounded youth
   And lifted, vaguely, his light lovely hair,
And that strange scar—the brother's hand, in truth
   Against him—as in distant days was there.
But now that brother look'd at his distress
With a remorse that changed to tenderness,
   And tried to raise him with a timid care.

And watch'd him many a moaning after-night,
   Through which the shine of spectral steel would go,

Through which lost armies would rise up and fight
    Lost battles, in the air—then waver slow
And haze-like down, and whiten toward the dust,
Leaving behind a little blood and rust
    And glory. Glory? Why, I do not know.

At last the War's fierce music left the wind,
    And they who answer'd to its infinite cries
With their whole breath were gone where God can find
    Them, when He searches land and sea and skies;
And Peace remain'd—a beautiful white vail,
Wrought by hurt hands that dropp'd off thin and pale,
    To hide the tears in wan, wet, restless eyes.

And the twin-brothers—one just from his wound—
    Talk'd of their brier-rose that would blossom yet,
Talk'd of the river with its far-back sound,
    Talk'd of their mother with a still regret,
And of the fairy boat she gave them both:
And then a sudden silence show'd them loath
    To talk of—what they did not quite forget.

Just then it happen'd that a pretty flash
    Of small spring-lightning made their window bright:

THE BROTHER'S HAND.

They saw a fluttering dress, a bright-plaid sash,
    A wide straw-hat, and loose hair falling quite
Half-way to eager feet. And so they guess'd,
Each in a shy half-dreaming way, the rest:
    They thought the girl was lovely? They were right.

Her face in glimpses came to haunt the two,
    Her voice was not what common voices are;
And soon the twin-born rivals darkly knew
    The old feud was not dead. They saw the scar
Out of its dreary quiet rise again:
The brother's hand was terrible and plain
    Against the brother, as in years afar.

She loved them both. Which most? I think that she—
    At least not yet—nor any other knew.
Sometimes she walk'd with Frederick by the sea,
    Sometimes she sung a tremulous song to Hugh,
And in a while, no doubt, began to know
That he was handsome, or she thought him so,
    And that his eyes, perhaps, were frankly blue.

Out with the darker brother once, a storm
    Broke sharply down the twilight. For a time

THE BROTHER'S HAND.

She clung to him. But, dry again and warm,
   Among their lamps she sung a sobbing rhyme
To her piano—and the gold-hair'd man—
Whose desolate music ended and began
   With a far, subtle, creeping, sea-like chime.

Then hush'd and went half-tearful to her room,
   Asking herself but this: "Which shall I choose?
Have I the saddest need of light or gloom?
   The fair one surely is too fair to lose:
Without him half the world were empty, and
Without his brother——if I understand,
   The dark one is too dark to quite refuse.

"And sometimes if I only glance at him,
   His richer, fiercer color seems to me
To make his stiller brother look as dim
   As a star looks by lightning. Let me be,
My star, with the white constant light you shed;
Fade out, my lightning, or else strike me dead.
   For star and lightning can but ill agree."

But something startled her brown window-bird,
   Nested below in perfume. As it flew

THE BROTHER'S HAND.

She heard her own name spoken, and she heard,
   Out in the wind, one ask: "Which of us two?
It is not well that both of us should stay.
Let her decide." In a bewilder'd way,
   Not knowing what she did, she whisper'd, "Hugh."

They heard below, and Frederick seem'd to laugh
   And said: "My boy, our paths again divide.
Your joy is great. If you could give me half,
   Enough were left. Good-by. The world is wide,
But all too narrow to hold you and me.
Good-by——and shall we let the Future be?
   Upon my faith you have a charming bride."

Next morning he was gone. And then, somehow,
   Hugh chanced in his vex'd dreamy way to throw
The yellow hair from his unquiet brow,
   And started from a glass which seem'd to show
That fearful scar, looking more deadly-white,
More like his brother's hand, too, since last night;
   Then scarlet suddenly it seem'd to grow.

She saw it: "Ah, you have a scar," she said.
   "How strange it is—and how much like a hand."

THE BROTHER'S HAND.

"It *is* a hand," he answered. "See how red
   It threatens now. It cut the gentle band
Between us while we yet were children." "Who?"
"We twins that called each other Fred and Hugh,
   And play'd beside a river in the sand."

A troubled paleness fell upon her face.
   She look'd at him an instant. "If I may?"
She said, and, bird-like, flutter'd from her place,
   And flush'd and doubted, and—I must not say
She kiss'd the scar. But I can say it grew
Yet deeper scarlet, and look'd darker too,
   And seem'd to move—motioning her away.

————The leaf-bloom of the Fall was in the woods—
   (The next day was to be their wedding-day.)
A cruel rain whirl'd down in pitiless floods
   And fretted the poor leaves that tried to stay
And wear their splendor for a little yet.
The butterflies were faded out and wet,
   Or else the wind had blown them all away.

The crimson-curtain'd, pleasant parlor glow'd
   With ferns and asters, and a sparkling fire;

THE BROTHER'S HAND.

The next-day's bride before the mirror show'd
    The trailing mistiness of a bride's attire.
And Hugh look'd at her, smiling from his dream:
He was not happy, quite, nor did he seem;
    Yet such sweet vanity he must admire.

She turn'd to take a letter that came in,
    And read it, and look'd at him as she read,
And threw it at his feet. "And be your sin,"
    She hoarsely whisper'd, "upon your own head."
"My sin?" "See there, and—say it is not true."
"I will not. All I say is this: if you
    Believe it—let to-morrow not begin!"

Then there were angry words, and—"Let us part,"
    She moan'd, and reach'd to him her frighten'd hand,
Thinking that he would hold it—to his heart—
    And kiss her pain away, as she had plann'd:
For she forgave him—what he had not done.
He answer'd: "As you please." And there was none
    To come between them, or to understand.

What then? The thistles blew across the rain,
    The gray, wet thorn-tree glimmer'd once and shook.

She thought: "If one should never come again—
  Should never come—after a bitter look?"
And—the dry asters from the mantel fell:
She brought no fresh ones for the vases. Well?
  And silence settled in his favorite book.

She did not thin her beauty with her tears,
  But was she tearless? Doubtless she was not.
But all the outward gladness of her years
  Was not because of one great grief forgot.
Loose hair and laughter, singing quick and sweet,
Follow'd about the green home-grass her feet,
  And quieted all wordless, kindly fears.

She had no mother. But her father said:
  "You are too hasty, little girl, I fear.
Hugh is a manly fellow; as for Fred——
  The villian! Hugh will come again, my dear,
Before the fashion of your dress shall change,
And we shall have our wedding." Was it strange?
  The dress grew quaint. And Hugh did not appear.

    ——Once at the sea-side, in an evening dance,
      She felt—and, fluttering, tried to fly away—

THE BROTHER'S HAND.

The bird-like terror of the snake-like glance.
   Poor, charméd little thing—and must it stay?
"Frederick?" "Well—yes." "Where is your
      brother, Hugh?"
"Am I my brother's keeper? Doubtless you
   Who wounded and deserted him, can say."

Hurt and bewilder'd, then she brokenly tried
   The secret of his letter to recall.
His letter? With feign'd anger he denied
   That he had written—any thing at all!
"What a mysterious piece of villiany!
Hugh never could have thought so ill of me.
   He did not read it?" Then he heard her fall.

—— It was the crowded room, and they must go
   Into the wide moonlighted air apart.
Where was his brother, then? He said, to know
   He would give up the last throb of his heart;
It was two years or more since he had heard
Of Hugh one word, one single precious word:
   Then broke into a cry that made her start.

By dim degrees he made himself grow dear,
   By seeming every thing his brother was.

THE BROTHER'S HAND.

Whatever in the other had been clear,
   In him she saw—darkly as in a glass.
At last, in some weird, subtle way, he grew
The shadow, or the very self, of Hugh.
 . And—well, the Summer wither'd from the grass.

What then? The asters in the vases glow'd
   Again; the parlor held the shining fire
Again; the mirror, three years older, show'd
   The trailing mistiness of a bride's attire;
And, this time, Frederick watch'd her from his dream.
He was not happy, quite, nor did he seem,
   Yet such fair vanity he must admire.

Once more the thistles blew across the rain,
   The gray, wet thorn-tree glimmer'd once and shook;
And then she thought: "If one should come again—
   Or should not come—after a bitter look!"
And then—a sudden voice, familiar-low,
And phantom-sweet, but heavily-bent and slow,
   Read out the silence of the old favorite book.

No matter. In a wedded year or two,
   In a far Western land a cottage rose,

THE BROTHER'S HAND.

With sand and sea and sea-shell shining through
   Its many windows—so the story goes.
Frederick was happy there. But his late bride
Had backward-yearning eyes, and sometimes sigh'd
   A little—as all women may? Who knows?

Once bitterly he ask'd: "What makes you sad?"
   She answer'd languidly: "Perhaps the sea.
I sometimes think it surely has gone mad:
   It foams and mutters till it frightens me.
Sometimes when it looks only golden, and
All things look golden in this Golden Land,
   Blackly below it threatens things to be."

And, as her childish words fail'd at her lip,
   From silks and spices and a foreign sail,
She saw a man drop from a landing ship
   As heavily as he had been a bale
Of precious merchant-freight. With the great light
Of the great evening smitten, he was bright—
   But all who look'd at him were dull and pale.

A life-boat brought him strangling to the coast.
   He motion'd them, in a despairing way,

To drown his body. For his soul was lost,
  He said: it shook him off and plunged away
From the dark deck into the gulfs below,
For utter loneliness. And he must go
  And find it, somewhere—for the Judgment Day.

Then he died, smiling.——Frederick and his wife
  Look'd at him and each other, and then wound
Their arms about him. What was calm or strife
  To him or them? What had they lost and found?
What thing was near? What things were gone afar?
With tears, and without words, they kiss'd the scar—
  His brother's hand against him all his life.

THE HIGHEST MOUNTAIN.

I know of a higher Mountain. Well?
  "Do the flowers grow on it?" No, not one.
"What is its name?" But I can not tell.
  "Where——?" Nowhere under the sun!

"Is it under the moon, then?" No, the light
  Has never touch'd it, and never can;
It is fashion'd and form'd of night, of night
  Too dark for the eyes of man.

Yet I sometimes think, if my Faith had proved
  As a grain of mustard seed to me,
I could say to this Mountain: "Be thou removed,
  And be thou cast in the sea!"

OFFERS FOR THE CHILD.

In the dim spaces of a dream, you see—
  Somewhere, perhaps, or else not anywhere,
(Remember in a dream what things may be)—
  I met a stranger with the whitest hair.

From his wide, wandering beard the snow-flakes
    whirl'd—
  (His face when young, no doubt, was much admired:)
His name was Atlas, and he held the world;
  I held a child—and both of us were tired.

'A handsome boy," he courteously said;
  "He pleases my old fancy. What fine eyes!"
"Yes, father, but he wearies me. My head
  Is aching, too, and—listen how he cries!"

"If you would let me take him"——and he spread
  All his fair laces and deep velvets wide;
Then hid them from my smile, and, in their stead,
  Sweet jewels and vague sums of gold he tried.

OFFERS FOR THE CHILD.

Then ships, all heavy with the scents and sounds
   Of many a sea, the stains of many a sun;
Then palaces, with empires for their grounds,
   Were slowly offer'd to me, one by one.

"Then take the world! It will amuse you. So,
   Watch while I move its wires." An instant, then,
He laugh'd. " Look, child, at this quick puppet-
      show:"
   I saw a rich land dusk with marching men.

"This puppet, with the smile inscrutable,
   You call The Emperor; these, Statesmen; these—
No matter; this, who just now plays the fool,
   Is "—— "Not our"—— "It is, madam, if you
      please!"*

"Hush!——" "Take the world and move them as
      you will!—
   Give me the boy."
                ——Then, shivering with affright,
I held the close cheek's dimples closer still,
   And bade the old Peddler—for I woke—good-night!

*186—

HER LAST GIFT.

Come here. I know while it was May
   My mouth was your most precious rose,
My eyes your violets, as you say.
   Fair words, as old as Love, are those.

I gave my flowers while they were sweet,
   And sweetly you have kept them, all
Through my slow Summer's great last heat
   Into the lonely mist of Fall.

Once more I give them. Put them by,
   Back in your memory's faded years—
Yet look at them, sometimes; and try,
   Sometimes, to kiss them through your tears.

I've dimly known, afraid to know,
   That you should have new flowers to wear;
Well, buds of rose and violets blow
   Before you in the unfolding air.

HER LAST GIFT.

So take from other hands, I pray,
   Such gifts of flowers as mine once gave:
I go into the dust, since they
   Can only blossom from my grave.

A SISTER OF MERCY.

There, by the man condemn'd to die, she read
  Christ's promise in the Crucifixion tale.
He moan'd a name——
              She dropp'd her cross and fled
From the long shadow of the veil!

And, as from her loosed convent coif she shook
  Her youthful hair's free length of beauty, he
Threw from his face the scarr'd and sinful look,
  And follow'd her across the sea!

There, in a Land of Distance vague with Spring,
  She, fair as that one morning-bud she wore,
Held him her frighten'd hand to take——the ring
  They found upon his prison floor!

"The ring was full of poison"—so they said;
  "A Sister of Mercy left it at his side!"
The gathering crowd must know the wretch was dead,
  Nor blame his jailer that he died.

A SISTER OF MERCY.

Perhaps their prisoner gray and ghastly lay;
  Perhaps the black-robed Sister, worn and bow'd,
Who pray'd there with that prisoner yesterday,
  Was at St. Mary's in her shroud.

Yet, in some Land of Distance full of Spring,
  Whither their Youth of Love had pass'd before,
He gave her hand the spirit of the ring
  They found upon his prison floor!

EARTH IN HEAVEN.

Somewhere, my friend, in the beautiful skies,
   Awaiting us lovely and clear,
We shall find all beauty that leaves our eyes
   So vacant in vanishing here:
Not the human alone has died
To go up and be glorified.

I shall find my childhood playing there
   In the grass where it used to play,
And see our red-birds brighten the air;
   Again as a girl I shall stray
On the hills where the snow-drops grew,
And hear the wild doves in the dew.

I shall feel the darkness dripping with rain
   On the old home-roof; I shall see
The white rose-bud in the yard again,
   And the sweet-brier climbing the tree,

EARTH IN HEAVEN.

With its pretty young blooms that fell
Below to be drown'd in the well.

And sometimes a night, with blossoming hours
   In a crescent's early gleam,
Will let a Dream flutter out of its flowers,
   With no other name but a Dream,
To my breast, with a timid grace
And wings o'er its blushing face.

Ah! you smile in the dark; you smile, and refuse
   My faith in these sweet faded things;
But I tell you I know that my soul would lose
   One-half of the strength in its wings
If these were not keeping their light,
As the angels in Heaven, to-night.

LAST WORDS.

OVER A LITTLE BED AT NIGHT.

GOOD-NIGHT, pretty sleepers of mine—
  I never shall see you again:
Ah, never in shadow nor shine;
  Ah, never in dew nor in rain!

In your small dreaming-dresses of white,
  With the wild-bloom you gather'd to-day
In your quiet shut hands, from the light
  And the dark you will wander away.

Though no graves in the bee-haunted grass,
  And no love in the beautiful sky,
Shall take you as yet, you will pass,
  With this kiss, through these tear-drops. Good-by!

With less gold and more gloom in their hair,
  When the buds near have faded to flowers,
Three faces may wake here as fair—
  But older than yours are, by hours!

LAST WORDS.

Good-night, then, lost darlings of mine—
I never shall see you again:
Ah, never in shadow nor shine;
Ah, never in dew nor in rain!

MY ARTIST.

[A. V. P.—*Nat.* 1864.]

So slight, and just a little vain
   Of eyes and amber-tinted hair
Such as you will not see again—
   To watch him at the window there,
Why, you would not suspect, I say,
The rising rival of Doré.

No sullen lord of foreign verse
   Such as great Danté yet he knows;
No Wandering Jew's long legend-curse
   On his light hand its darkness throws;
Nor has the Bible suffer'd much,
So far, from his irreverent touch.

Yet, can his restless pencil lack
   A master Fancy, weird and strong
In black-and-white—but chiefly black!—
   When at its call such horrors throng?

MY ARTIST.

What Fantasies of Fairyland
More shadowy were ever plann'd!

But giants and enchantments make
   Not all the glory of his Art:
His vast and varied power can take
   In real things a real part.
His latest pictures here I see:
Will you not look at some with me?

First, "Alexander." From his wars,
   With arms of awful length he seems
To reach some very-pointed stars,
   As if "more worlds" were in his dreams!
But, hush—the Artist tells us why:
"You read—'His hands could touch the sky.'"

Here—mark how marvelous, how new!—
   Above a drowning ship, at night,
Close to the moon the sun shines, too,
   While lightnings show in streaks of white——
Still, should my eyes grow dim, ah, then
Their tears will wet those sinking men!

There in wild weather, quite forlorn,
   And queer of cloak, and grim of hat,

With locks that might be better shorn,
   High on a steeple—who is that?
"It is the man who—I forget—
Stood on a tower in the wet."

His faults? He yet is young, you know—
   Four with his last year's butterflies.
But think what wonders books may show
   When the new Tennysons arise!
For fame that he might illustrate
Let poets be content to wait!

IN THE GRAVEYARD.

THE sweetness dropp'd from the cherry-blooms
    Over the sleep that is never stirr'd,
And the twilight droop'd on her purple plumes,
    And flutter'd and moan'd, like a dying bird,
Till I hid my face in the scented glooms.

The grasses were damp where the thorns had grown;
    The bats flew close to the mouldering staves;
Some wild, white buds, with a windy moan,
    Fell with their faces against the graves,
And the moss-veils hung on the broken stone.

Out of the dim and dusky sky
    A golden blossoming broke ere long,
And glitter'd and fell on the spring-woods nigh,
    Where a dove was hushing her sleepy song;
And we were together, the dead and I.

"The heart above, with its breaking strings,
   Wails dissonant music, stormy or slow;
But ah! what a beautiful stillness clings,
   Sweet Death," I said, " to the hearts below,
That are touch'd with the calm of your pallid wings.

"But is memory still where the vanished go?"
   Then I thought of a tender dream of the past,
That faded and fell in a passionate woe,
   Like a lotus-flower in a poison'd blast;
And I stared in the shadow and said, " You know.

"Come out of your silence once more, and seem
   The thing that I loved in the years afar,
While the wild-bird flutters and sings in its dream,
   And the yellow bloom of the evening star
Drops, as of old, in the whispering stream."

You came, and I saw the tremulous breeze
   Blow the loose brown hair about your head;
You came, thro' a murmur of melodies;
   You came, for love can awaken the dead;
You came, and stood by the cherry-trees.

IN THE GRAVEYARD.

You came, and your white hand was not cold,
    And your quiet eyes, they were not dim;
And we watched the moon-rise dripping with gold,
    While the waters chanted a vesper hymn,
And your lip was flush'd with the tales it told.

I could see the wings of the sun's pet birds,
    I could hear the delicate sigh of the shells,
And the giant cry of the seas in your words;
    Yet others had heard but the distant bells,
And seen but the glimmer of rocks and herds.

I whisper'd like one that is not awake:
    "Does sorrow die with our dying breath?
Did it drop from your life like a wounded snake,
    When the dust of your beauty was touch'd with death?
Oh, tell me, oh, tell me, for love's sweet sake.

"Say, is memory still, where the vanished go?
    Say, Presence out of the spicy zones—
Let your sweet lip whisper the secret low,
    While I wait by the mosses and broken stones:
Ah, you hide in your silence, and yet you know."

THE END OF THE RAINBOW.

May you go to find it? You must, I fear;
   Ah, lighted young eyes, could I show you how——
"Is it past those lilies that look so near?"
   It is past all flowers. Will you listen, now?

The pretty new moons faded out of the sky,
   The bees and butterflies out of the air,
And sweet wild songs would flutter and fly
   Into wet dark leaves and the snow's white glare.

There were winds and shells full of lonesome cries,
   There were lightnings and mists along the way,
And the deserts would glitter against my eyes,
   Where the beautiful phantom-fountains play.

At last, in a place very dusty and bare,
   Some little dead birds I had petted to sing,
Some little dead flowers I had gather'd to wear,
   Some wither'd thorns and an empty ring,

THE END OF THE RAINBOW.

Lay scatter'd. My fairy story is told.
(It does not please her: she has not smiled.)
What is it you say?—Did I find the gold?
Why, I found the End of the Rainbow, child!

TWO BLUSH-ROSES.

A BLUSH-ROSE lay in the summer;
   There were golden lights in the sky,
And a woman saw the blossom
   As she stood with her lover nigh.

A band in the flowering distance
   Play'd a dreamy Italian air,
Like a memory changed to music,
   And it drifted everywhere.

'T was an exiled love of its Southland,
   That air, and its delicate wails
Were only the wandering echoes
   Of the songs of nightingales.

"I love you," he tenderly whisper'd;
   "I love you," she answer'd as low:
And the music grew sweeter and sweeter,
   Because it had listen'd, I know.

But she look'd at the rose in the summer,
   And said, with a tremulous tear,
"The love that now beats in my bosom
   Will bloom in a blush-rose next year."

A blush-rose lay in the summer;
   There were golden lights in the sky,
And a woman saw the blossom—
   As she stood with her lover nigh.

The band in the flowering distance
   Play'd the dreamy Italian air,
Like a memory changed to music,
   And it drifted everywhere.

"I love you," he tenderly whisper'd;
   "I love you," she timidly said:
And the music grew sadder and sadder,
   And the blush-rose before them dropp'd dead.

Then he knew that the music remember'd,
   And knew the love that had beat
Last year in her beautiful bosom
   Lay dead in the rose at his feet.

OF A PARTING.

Under a calm of stars, my own,
   Under a drooping crescent light,
You go, while fairy sounds are blown
Out of the dreams of winds, my own—
   You go across the night;
But on some far-off strand of sunrise
   Our hearts meet in a radiant bliss,
         Not damp, like this!

You go; the calm of stars must go,
   The crescent light, the fairy sounds;
Billows of cloud will overflow
The golden skies: but you must go.
   And in its stormy rounds
The dark will hear low, fluttering voices
   Cry in my heart, like lonesome birds,
         For your sweet words.

You go, and twilights made for love
   Will gloom between us, dim with dew;
The spring-loosed music of the dove
Will search the emerald woods for love,

OF A PARTING.

And I will long for you,
Among the blue and pearly blossoms
  Far on the mossy hills, alone,
      My own, my own.

But you must loose my hands and go.
  Haste with those tremulous words of pain,
For I, most loved of all, I know
(The thought is full of tears) some go
  And never come again;
So wait, and let me look forever
  Into the tenderness that lies
      In those deep eyes.

Ah! you are gone; and I—I hold
  My vacant arms to all who part,
And weep for them, and long to fold
Those strangers close, and say: "I hold
  Your sorrow in my heart;"
But look—the calm of stars is o'er us,
  And we go toward their lighted shore,
      And part no more.

1861.

A CHILD'S FIRST SIGHT OF SNOW.

Oh, come and look at his blue, sweet eyes,
   As, through the window, they glance around
And see the glittering white surprise
   The Night has laid on the ground!

This beautiful Mystery you have seen,
   So new to your life, and to mine so old,
Little wordless Questioner —— "What does it mean?"
   Why, it means, I fear, that the world is cold.

A LILY OF THE NILE.

Who was the beautiful woman whose lover
   Once left her this dead old flower, did you say?
Well, perhaps that is she in the picture over
   The vase with the flowers which you gather'd to-day.

The one with the deep strange dress, that is flowing
   All purple and pearls through each stiffen'd fold,
And the band on her forehead, whose dusk-red glowing
   Shoots into great sharp thorns of gold.

Never mind the light. You will see, to-morrow,
   That, with eyes raised darkly and lips close-prest,
She is giving away her awful sorrow
   To the snake she keeps at her breast!

"And who was her lover?" Why, that may be he, there,
   In the other picture glimmering nigh—
Yes, the handsome and wretched man you see there,
   Falling against his sword to die.

A LILY OF THE NILE.

Will he die for *her*, do you say? (Ah, will he?)
  No doubt he has often told her so!
"Did it bloom far away, this crumbling lily?"
  Very far——and so long ago.

And who gave it to *me?*
                      ——So the wither'd story
  I've dream'd by the twilight all this while,
For some vanish'd blossom's day of glory,
  Is your truth, my Lily of the Nile.

For the beautiful woman *is* slowly dying
  Of a snake as plain as this to my sight;
And her lover who gave her this flower is lying
  On the edge of a sword to-night.

A DISENCHANTMENT.

And thou wast but a breathing May
   Embodied by delicious dreams,
And drifted o'er my wandering way
   On fancy's swift and shining streams.
Thine eyes were only violets,
   Thy lips but buds of crimson bloom,
Thy hair, coiled sunshine—vain regrets!
   Thy soul, a brief perfume.

And when the time of mists and chills
   Fell where the sweet wild roses grew,
And took them from the shadowy hills,
   It took my lovely vision too;
And when I came again to find
   The charm which used to fill the air,
A sorrow struck me mute and blind—
   Thou wast not anywhere!

Yet something met me in thy place,
   Something, they said, with looks like thine,
With tresses full of golden grace
   And lips flush'd red with beauty's wine;

A DISENCHANTMENT.

With voice of silvery swells and falls
   And dreamy eyes still sweetly blue—
But, then, the reptile's nature crawls
   Beneath the rainbow's hue.

Woman, all things below, above,
   Look pale and drear and glimmering now,
For I have loved thee with a love
   Whose passionate deeps such things as thou
May never sound. And, with a moan,
   The chill'd tide of that love has rolled
Above my heart, and made it stone,
   And oh, so cold, so cold!

I saw thee by a magic lamp
   Whose warm and gorgeous blaze is gone,
And o'er me shivers, gray and damp,
   The dimness of the real's dawn.
Oh, I am like to one who stands
   Where late a vision smiled in air,
And murmurs, with outstretching hands,
   "Where is my Angel—where?"

THE FLOWERS IN THE GROUND.

UNDER the coffin-lid there are roses:
    They bud like dreams in the sleep of the dead;
And the long, vague dark that around them closes
    Is flush'd and sweet with their glory of red.

From the buried seeds of love they blossom,
    All crimson-stain'd from its blood they start;
And each sleeper wears them on his bosom,
    Clasp'd over the pallid dust of his heart.

When the Angel of Morning shall shake the slumber
    Away from the graves with his lighted wings,
He will gather thoses roses, an infinite number,
    And bear them to Heaven, the beautiful things!

QUESTIONS OF THE HOUR.

"Do angels wear white dresses, say?
   Always, or only in the summer? Do
Their birthdays have to come like mine, in May?
   Do they have scarlet sashes then, or blue?

"When little Jessie died last night,
   How could she walk to Heaven—it is so far?
How did she find the way without a light?
   There was n't even any moon or star.

"Will she have red or golden wings?
   Then will she have to be a bird, and fly?
Do they take men like presidents and kings
   In hearses with black plumes clear to the sky?

"How old is God? Has he gray hair?
   Can He see yet? Where did He have to stay
Before—you know—he had made—Anywhere?
   Who does He pray to—when He has to pray?

QUESTIONS OF THE HOUR.

"How many drops are in the sea?
   How many stars?——well, then, you ought to know
How many flowers are on an apple-tree?
   How does the wind look when it does n't blow?

"Where does the rainbow end? And why
   Did—Captain Kidd—bury the gold there? When
Will this world burn? And will the firemen try
   To put the fire out with the engines then?

"If you should ever die, may we
   Have pumpkins growing in the garden, so
My fairy godmother can come for me,
   When there's a prince's ball, and let me go?

"Read Cinderella just once more——
   What makes—men's other wives—so mean?" I know
That I was tired, it may be cross, before
   I shut the painted book for her to go.

Hours later, from a child's white bed
   I heard the timid, last queer question start:
"Mamma, are you—my stepmother?" it said.
   The innocent reproof crept to my heart.

GASLIGHT AND STARLIGHT.

THOSE flowers of flame that blossom at night
    From the dust of the city, along the street,
And wreathe rich rooms with their leaves of light,
    Were dropping their tremulous bloom at my feet.

And the men whose names by the crowd are known,
    And the women uplifted to share their place—
Some of them bright with their jewels alone,
    Some of them brighter with beauty and grace—

Were around me under the flashing rays,
    All seeming, I thought as I saw them there,
To ask the throng, in their pleased, mute ways,
    For its bow, or its smile, or at least its stare.

But, faint with the odors that floated about,
    And tired of the glory the few can win,
I turned to the window: the darkness without
    Struck heavily on the glitter within,

Still the glare behind me haunted my brain,
    And I thought: "They are blest who are shining so;"
But a voice replied: "You are blinded and vain—
    Such triumph when highest is often low.

"For some," it said, with a slow, sad laugh,
    "Who wear so proudly their little names,
Have leant on the People, as on a staff
    To help them up to their selfish fames.

"And others yet—it is hard to know—
    Have crawl'd through the dust to their sunny hour,
To crawl the same in its warmth and glow
    And hiss the snake in the colors of Power.

"Yet it is comfort to feel, through the whole,
    They only look great, in God's calm eyes,
Who lean on the still, grand strength of the soul
    And climb toward the pure, high light of the skies."

A DREAM'S AWAKENING.

Shut in a close and dreary sleep,
   Lonely and frightened and oppress'd
I felt a dreadful serpent creep,
   Writhing and crushing, o'er my breast.

I woke and knew my child's sweet arm,
   As soft and pure as flakes of snow,
Beneath my dream's dark, hateful charm,
   Had been the thing that tortured so.

And, in the morning's dew and light
   I seem'd to hear an angel say,
"The Pain that stings in Time's low night
   May prove God's Love in higher day."

TALK ABOUT GHOSTS.

[AT BED-TIME.]

"Each of us carries within him a future ghost."

WHAT *is* a ghost? "It is something white,
   (And I guess it goes barefooted, too,)
That comes from the graveyard in the night,
   When the doors are lock'd, and breaks right through."
      What does it do?

"Oh, it frightens people ever so much,
   And goes away when the chickens crow;
And—does n't steal any spoons, or touch
   One thing that is n't its own, you know."
      Who told you so?

"Somebody—every body, almost;
   Or I knew, myself, when this world begun.
Not even a General could kill a ghost——
   I wish the Lord had never made one.
      They hate the sun!"

TALK ABOUT GHOSTS.

No, sweetest of all wee brown-eyed girls,
   They love the light—'t is the dark they fear;
Love riches and power, love laces and pearls;
   Love—all the preacher calls vanity here.
      This much is clear.

"Do they love to be dead?" I can but tell
   That few of them greatly love to die:
Perhaps they doubt whether all is well
   In the place where ghosts——yes, "up in the sky."
      You wonder why?

They love their clothes (and want to keep dress'd :)
   Whether new and prettily white and red,
Or gray and ragged, 't is hard, at best,
   To take them off—though the prayers are said—
      And go to bed.

A YEAR.—MDCCCLX.

My spirit saw a scene
Whose splendors were so terrible and bright
   That the infinitude of mist between
The earth and sky scarce saved its eagle-sight
From being blasted. In the middle night
   He stood, the Guardian Angel of the Years:
His wings—that could extend their quenchless light
   Across eternity, and rock the spheres
With their immortal strength—were folded now,
Like a still veil of glory, on his brow.

One fiery star and vast,
A gem to note the year, forever more
   Burn'd in his ancient crown; and fierce and fast
Escaped the flame from out the one he wore,
Whose dimness vaguely settled on each shore
   Along the seas of space; and, pale and lone,
But kingly with the solemn pride of yore,
   Clinching the grandeur of a shadowy throne,
As if to hold his royalty from Death,
One lean'd beside him with an icy breath.

Nor earth, nor heaven will save
Us from the Doom which claim'd that mighty thing;
But, then, who fears or thinks upon the grave—
That narrow dark through which the free may spring
To the wide light beyond? Who seeks to cling
With coward grasp to fetters and to strife?
Death is the only halcyon whose white wing
Can still the billows of a restless life.
Yet, were the present peace, the future woe,
New storms are better than a calm we know.

He said, "My sceptre cast
Its shadows far as God's dominions lie;
Storms blew their thunder-trumpets as I pass'd,
And lightnings follow'd me about the sky.
I clasped th' unwilling worlds and heard them sigh
Against my breast with all their winds and waves;
Ay, as my victor chariot hurried by
Sun, star, and comet, like affrighted slaves,
Flung portions of their measured light below
Its silent wheels to make a triumph glow

"I passed you radiant crowd
Of constellations, and there knelt beside
The Cross upon whose like a God has bow'd;
I met the mourning Pleiades, and cried

To their lost sister in th' unanswering tide
  Of night; I struck weird music from the Lyre,
And humbled old Orion's sullen pride,
  Who lean'd against his cimeter of fire,
And, with submissive reverence and mute,
Acknowledged my imperious salute.

    "Look, look—for all his deeds
Must pass before the sight of him who dies;
  Mine crowd the infinite spaces—but man needs
Not to be told of those whose scenery lies
Beyond the bounds he knows, for his dim eyes
  See but the things I have around him wrought;
He will not hear the dirge that soon must rise
  For me in all the myriad realms his thought
May visit, only by the hazy route
That glimmers round the reeling sails of Doubt.

    " The shadow of his world,
Like a dark canvas spread before me seems:
  There hides the hermit West, with cataracts whirl'd
Among the rocks, watching their foamy beams;
There are the groves of myrrh, and diamond gleams,
  Where—fair as if it erewhile floated to
Its own warm poets, in their lotus dreams,
  As an ideal Aidenn, and there grew

Into reality—the Orient lies
Close to the morn 'mid birds of Paradise.

  " There ice-mail'd warders keep
The gates of silence by the auroral rays
 Which fall above the cold-press'd North asleep,
Like a proud, pallid Queen, in the rich blaze
Of colored lamps, upon whose bosom weighs
 A dreary vision; and there, too, the sweet,
Sun-worshipp'd South in languid beauty stays,
 Like a sultana, caring but to meet
Her fiery lover 'mid her gorgeous bowers,
And, as his bride, be crown'd with orange flowers.

  " And, over all, there moves
The phantasm of my life. With joy and dread
 I see it passing, and my memory proves
Its truth to nature. Roses white and red,
Whose leaves into the winds have long been shed,
 And tremulous lily-bells, and jasmine blooms
Are there, as they had risen from the dead,
 So like their early selves their lost perfumes
Seem blown about them, and I hear the breeze
That used to kiss them sing old melodies.

  " Above, the changing sky
Shows wonder-pictures to my fading eyes:

Now, the black armies of the clouds march by,
Now rainbows bloom, now golden moons arise.
Below, how varied too: now glitter lies
   On gorgeous jewels, bridal-flowers and mirth;
Now mourners pass, and fill the air with sighs,
   To hide their coffins in the yawning earth;
Now, with a pallid face and frenzied mind,
Cold, starving wretches ask if God is blind!

      " Now reels a nightmare throne
From the crush'd bosom of the Sicilies,
   The South's brief dream of blood wakes in the sun;
Glad winds sing on the blue Italian seas,
And glad men bless me by their olive-trees;
   Now, in the clouds above a younger land,
With awful eyes fix'd on its destinies,
   The frowning souls of its dead Glorious stand
And see a fiery madness, that would blast
God's miracle of freedom, kindling fast."

      He fix'd a dark, wild look
On his celestial watcher, as in hate;
   Then grasp'd him, till his passionless grandeur
      shook,
And mutter'd: " Spirit, see the fate of fate
I've left upon mortality's estate.

A YEAR.

And thou didst suffer all this ruin, thou
Whose office was to warn me; 'tis too late
  For me to give thee these reproaches now,
For I am growing cold—my deeds are done,
And thou shouldst blush for them, thou guilty one.

    "I tell thee, thou shalt hear—
For, Guardian Angel of the Years, I swear
  Thou art a traitor to thy God! And fear
A traitor's fate, if thou again shalt dare
Neglect thy task. Then aid him who shall bear
  The sceptre I resign to quench all wrong,
And kindle right—or, when I meet thee where
  None may evade the truth, my oath, as strong
As aught except thy brother Lucifer's curse,
Shall drag thee down to share his doom or worse!

    "Mortals, I go, I go.
Yet, though we part, it is to meet again;
  My ghost will come with noiseless step and slow
Along the twilights, whispering of my reign;
And, in the night-times, oft a mystic strain
  Shall strike your sleep, and ye shall know my tone,
Singing remembered airs, not all in vain,
  And chorus them with an unconscious moan;

And I must witness of you in the day
When earth and heaven shall melt in fire away."

  He drew the dark around
His ghastly face—the nations sigh'd farewell;
 He stagger'd from his throne—an awful sound
Rolled down from every system's every bell,
That toll'd together once to make his knell,
 And the resplendent crown-star, that had flash'd
On the lone Angel's brow, grew black and fell—
 Shattering among six thousand more it crash'd.
I ask'd: "How many stay for him to wear?"
I woke: and Midnight's silence fill'd the air.

ON A WEDDING DAY.

I look far-off across the blue,
   Still distance vague with woods and Spring—
The Earth is sweet with buds and dew;
   The birds their early carols sing.

I look, and somehow wish the hours
   Held calm and sun and bloom alone:
No fallen leaves, no wither'd flowers,
   No storm, no wreck, no mist, no moan;

No painted palms of air on sand,
   No poisons where the spice-winds blow,
No dark shapes haunting sea and land—
   But wherefore am I dreaming so?

It is because this music swells
   Across the lighted April day—
Because I hear your bridal bells,
   Fair girl, a thousand miles away.

ON A WEDDING DAY.

Yes, lovely in a holy place,
   Enchanted by my dream you rise:
The young blush-roses on your face,
   The timid darkness in your eyes.

And, golden on your hand, I see
   The glitter of a sacred thing:
I wish some Fairy, friend, may be
   Slave of the ring—your wedding ring!

THE DOVE AND THE ANGEL.

THE roses and stars were in blossom:
　　She leant by the lattice alone,
And a pet dove, white as a lily,
　　Flew out of the night with a moan,
And nestled down close in her bosom,
　　To hide from the wound in its own.

Tears rain'd on the snow of its plumage,
　　Tears rain'd on the golden moonshine;
"Ah, beautiful, tremulous darling,"
　　She murmured, "my life is like thine—
Only I have no bosom to fly to,
　　My bird, as you fly into mine."

The south-moon dropp'd under the shadow,
　　Yet she stay'd to remember and weep,
Till—what was the wonderful Presence,
　　So quiet and holy and deep,
That stole thro' the dreams of the roses,
　　Till they shook out their sweetness in sleep?

THE DOVE AND THE ANGEL.

Ah, an Angel that once was a mortal
  Flew out of the glories unknown,
And, like the white dove from the darkness
  That came to her love with its moan,
She nestled down close in his bosom,
  And hid from the wound in her own.

HER TALK WITH A REDBIRD.

[AT MORNING BEFORE SUNRISE.]

"THE only things in the world awake,
   And I for grief as for gladness you,
Let us be quiet. We should not shake
   The beautiful dimness from the dew.

"It is early to you, to me it is late.
   You rise in bloom toward the morning light;
I stand in the thorn's sharp shadow and wait
   For strength to crawl away from the night.

"Oh, Bird, flush'd Bird, you can sing and fly.
   For the song I hear and the wings I see,
I would give you—my soul and its share in the sky;
   And I would be you and you should be me.

"They would tell my children their mother was dead.
   'Never mind, she was tired and pale,' they would say,
'But here is a Bird, so pretty and red,
   'In your trees——to cry might scare it away!'"

MY WEDDING RING.

My heart stirr'd with its golden thrill
   And flutter'd closer up to thine,
In that blue morning of the June
   When first it clasp'd thy love and mine.

In it I see the little room,
   Rose-dim and hush'd with lilies still,
Where the old silence of my life
   Turn'd into music with "I will."

Oh, I would have my folded hands
   Take it into the dust with me:
All other little things of mine
   I'd leave in the bright world with thee.

A FALLING STAR.

Just then, upon its wings of fire,
    A star went flying by,
And vanish'd o'er the waves of cloud,
    A sea-bird of the sky!

To-night there ring within my heart
    Old half-forgotten chimes,
Whose mournful music memory caught
    Among its nursery-rhymes.

In those sweet years I've heard them say
    No wish could be in vain,
If it were form'd while flash'd thro' Heaven
    A meteor's sudden train.

Ah, then I only wish'd to catch
    The blue-birds on the hill,
Or, with bare feet to wander down
    Some shady woodland rill.

STONE FOR A STATUE.

LEAVE what is white for whiter use.
    For such a purpose as your own
Would be a dreary jest, a harsh abuse,
    A bitter wrong to snowy stone.

Let the pure marble's silence hold
    Its unshaped gods, and do not break
Those hidden images divine and old,
    To-day, for one mean man's small sake!

A BIRD'S WING AND A SOUL'S.

FOR MY SISTER AND BROTHER.

This small bright wing, that used to fly
   In far Kentucky's summer light
And lift clear music toward the sky,
   Lies full of tears to-night.

Wild little memory of the woods
   In whose dark paths we loved to go,
When the old hills were flush'd with buds
   Or pallid with the snow:

I kiss you, tenderly and fast—
   For her, the beautiful and dear,
Between whose lips and mine have pass'd
   The dim waves of a year;

For him through whose dark, careless hair
   The shadows of the palm-trees play—
Perchance in warm Pacific air
   He thinks of us to-day.

A BIRD'S WING AND A SOUL'S.

Ah, were I but the light, free bird
  That wore you through old woodland glooms,
Familiar leaves should soon be stirr'd
  With my returning plumes.

But that wild, wingéd thing is dust
  Where wither'd falls have dropp'd and blown,
And my wild, wingéd thoughts, I trust,
  Can fly on love alone.

FALLEN ANGELS.

They were to be the fairest ever known
  In the sphere of unstain'd Art, and to hold the high,
    far places
Among the shapes of Beauty born of stone,
  With divinest lift of wings and divinest calm of
    faces.

The sculptor started backward with a cry,
  And he pass'd across his eyes his piteous, worn hands
    slowly:—
Was this his great white vision from the sky,
  Standing palpable in marble, yet all radiant and
    holy?

He saw his days, his nights, his passions there,
  And his strength—a giant image that seem'd wrest-
    ling with its stillness—
Imprison'd in one wide hush of despair,
  At the feet of Fallen Angels, staring back with
    empty chillness!

TO MARIAN ASLEEP.

The full moon glimmers still and white,
   Where yonder shadowy clouds unfold;
The stars, like children of the Night,
   Lie with their little heads of gold
On her dark lap: nor less divine,
And brighter, seems your own on mine.

My darling, with your snowy sleep
   Folded around your dimpled form,
Your little breathings calm and deep,
   Your mother's arms and heart are warm;
You wear as lilies in your breast
The dreams that blossom from your rest.

Ah, must your clear eyes see ere long
   The mist and wreck on sea and land,
And that old haunter of all song,
   The mirage hiding in the sand?
And will the dead leaves in the frost
Tell you of song and summer lost?

And shall you hear the ghastly tales
  From the slow, solemn lips of Time—
Of Wrong that wins, of Right that fails,
  Of trampled Want and gorgeous Crime,
Of Splendor's glare in lighted rooms
And Famine's moan in outer glooms?

Of armies in their red eclipse
  That mingle on the smoking plain;
Of storms that dash our mighty ships
  With silks and spices through the main;
Of what it costs to climb or fall—
Of Death's great Shadow ending all?

But, baby Marian, do I string
  The dark with darker rhymes for you,
Forgetting that you came in Spring,
  The child of sun and bloom and dew,
And that I kiss'd, still fresh to-day,
The rosiest bud of last year's May?

Forgive me, pretty one: I know,
  Whatever sufferings onward lie,
Christ wore his crown of thorns below
  To gain his crown of light on high;
And when the lamp's frail flame is gone,
Look up: the stars will still shine on.

A PRESIDENT AT HOME.*

I pass'd a President's House to-day——
   "A President, mamma, and what is that?"
Oh, it is a man who has to stay
   Where bowing beggars hold out the hat
For something—a man who has to be
The Captain of every ship that we
Send with our darling flag to the sea—
The Colonel at home who has to command
Each marching regiment in the land.

This President now has a single room,
   That is low and not much lighted, I fear;
Yet the butterflies play in the sun and gloom
   Of his evergreen avenue, year by year;
And the child-like violets up the hill
Climb, faintly wayward, about him still;
And the bees blow by at the wind's wide will;

* At North Bend, Ohio River—the tomb of General Harrison.

And the cruel river, that drowns men so,
Looks pretty enough in the shadows below.

Just one little fellow (named Robin) was there,
   In a red Spring vest, and he let me pass
With that charming-careless, high-bred air
   Which comes of serving the great. In the grass
He sat, half-singing, with nothing to do——
No, I did not see the President too:
His door was lock'd (what I say is true),
And he was asleep, and has been, it appears,
Like Rip Van Winkle, asleep for years!

AN EAGLE'S PLUME FROM PALESTINE.

LEAVING the summer in the palms asleep
For lonely circles in the upper deep—
   Leaving the wild crusader's risen blood,
   That stands in many a crimson-stainéd bud,
As if to make a gentle guard of flowers,
   To keep the memory of the Holy Cross
Safe from the dark hands of unholy powers—
   Leaving the valley lilies and the moss:
Far up the silence of that Eastern sky,
   Whose suns and stars are haunted by the shine
   Left by the death-smile of a God, 'twas thine
To feel the vastness of infinity!

Phantoms of olive-trees, old cedar glooms,
A sacred stream—with tremulous, snowy plumes
   Bearing the Father's blessing from above,
   Shaped in the timid likeness of a dove—
And many solemn things, before me sweep,
   Call'd up by thee, thou that hast sailed far noons,
And lain against a lonesome mountain sleep
   Close to the golden-lighted Asian moons;

Yet, dusk enchanter, saddest of the sights,
   Which thy still wizardry has come to bring,
   Seems the dread picture of a falling wing—
A flying farewell to the sunward heights!

A falling wing—ah, even when it glows
With little fires and burns down from a rose,
   It must resist its sinking, with a pain
   That is sublime—a wish to rise again:
But when its place has been above the cloud,
   Where its high strength has dared the storm afar,
Then feels a downward weakness, slow and proud
   It drops—as grandly as an unsphered star,
Whose arms of light strive with their utmost powers
   To hold a place in heaven; and thus dropp'd thine,
   Dead eagle of the skies of Palestine,
And thus drop many in this world of ours!

A CHAIN FROM VENICE.

She stretches dimpled arms of snow;
   A glad smile lights her baby eyes:
My little beauty, would you know
   The story of your shining prize?

It is a poet's golden thought
   Of you, that glitters like your hair,
Of rich Venetian sunlight wrought
   Far in the South's enchanted air.

Ah, if you stay from Heaven to learn
   The years before you lying dim,
You'll think, my darling, in return,
   A thought as beautiful of him.

A WALK TO MY OWN GRAVE.

[WITH THREE CHILDREN.]

THERE! do not stop to cry.
   "The path is long?—we walk so slow?"
But we shall get there by and by.
   Every step that we go
   Is one step nearer, you know:
And your mother's grave will be
Such a pretty place to see.

"Will there be marble there,
   With doves, or lambs, or lilies?" No.
Keep white yourselves. Why should you care
   If they *are* as white as snow,
   When the lilies can not blow,
And the doves can never moan,
Nor the lambs bleat—in the stone?

You want some *flowers?* Oh!
   We shall not find them on the way.

A WALK TO MY OWN GRAVE.

Only a few brier-roses grow,
    Here and there, in the sun, I say.
    It is dusty and dry all day,
But at evening there is shade,
And——you will not be afraid?

Ah, the *flowers?* Surely, yes.
    At the end there will be a few.
    "Violets? Violets?" So I guess,
    And a little grass and dew;
    And some birds—you want them *blue?*
And a spring, too, as I think,
Where we will rest and drink.

Now kiss me and be good,
    For you can go back home and play.
This is my grave here in the wood,
    Where I, for a while, must stay.
    Wait—will you always pray,
Though you *are* sleepy, at night?
There! do not forget *me*—quite.

Keep the baby sweetly drest,
    And give him milk and give him toys;

A WALK TO MY OWN GRAVE.

Rock him, as I did, to his rest,
  And never make any noise,
  Brown-eyed girl and blue-eyed boys,
Until he wakes. Good-by,
And——do not stop to cry!

PARIS.

[JANUARY, 1871.]

Speak! Dying, that never can be dead!
  Speak! O wounded, and wan, and wasted!
"Blood is better than wine," she said—
  "Famine the sweetest food I have tasted.

"Pallor is brighter than bloom, and scars
  Than my old jewels have made me fairer.
When the Vapor put out my lamps, the stars
  Gave me a surer light and a rarer.

"My flowers were false, my glory was shame,
  My Life was Death, in my years of pleasure.
Divine from my sorrow my Beauty came—
  Safe in my ashes shall shine my treasure."

AN AFTER-POEM.

You will read, or you will not read,
   That the lilies are whitest after they wither;
That the fairest buds stay shut in the seed,
   Though the bee in the dew say "Come you up
      hither."

You have seen, if you were not blind,
   That the moon can be crowded into a crescent,
And promise us light that we never can find
   When the midnights are wide and yellow and
      pleasant.

You will know, or you will not know,
   That the seas to the sun can fling their foam only,
And keep all their terrible waters below
   With the jewels and dead men quiet and lonely.

WITH DISTANT ECHOES.

*"Of far-off, old, unhappy times,
And battles long ago."*
— **WORDSWORTH.**

HEARING THE BATTLE.—July 21, 1861.

One day in the dreamy summer,
  On the Sabbath hills, from afar
We heard the solemn echoes
  Of the first fierce words of war.

Ah, tell me, thou veilèd Watcher
  Of the storm and the calm to come,
How long by the sun or shadow
  Till these noises again are dumb.

And soon in a hush and glimmer
  We thought of the dark, strange fight,
Whose close in a ghastly quiet
  Lay dim in the beautiful night.

Then we talk'd of coldness and pallor,
  And of things with blinded eyes
That stared at the golden stillness
  Of the moon in those lighted skies;

And of souls, at morning wrestling
　In the dust with passion and moan,
So far away at evening
　In the silence of worlds unknown.

But a delicate wind beside us
　Was rustling the dusky hours,
As it gather'd the dewy odors
　Of the snowy jessamine-flowers.

And I gave you a spray of the blossoms,
　And said: "I shall never know
How the hearts in the land are breaking,
　My dearest, unless you go."

THE CHRISTMAS TREE OUT-OF-DOORS.

" THE Saint of Christmas leaves his charmèd treasures
   Only in homes where there is gold to buy.
What though small voices ask for childish pleasures,
   Among the poor—he makes them no reply.

" Ah well, his great close furs shut out their crying;
   He can not drive in narrow streets, we know,
Or find his way to hearths in darkness lying "—
   A woman thought, and look'd into the snow.

When, greener than all Springs can make their greenness,
   A giant Tree grew in the freezing air,
And from the far sky's beautiful sereneness
   Strange shapes of wondrous calmness gather'd there.

Some, through their Peace, show'd dimly the scarr'd faces
   That fell, in moldering battle-pits, away:
These brought fair fruits from ever-shining places,
   That children of dead soldiers might be gay.

THE CHRISTMAS TREE OUT-OF-DOORS.

Next, shadows of worn living mothers slowly—
  From the thick night below—came, sad to see,
And, with a tenderness most sweet and holy,
  Hung pretty toys on the enchanted Tree.

Then, as a dove, a radiance descended,
  And show'd these children of the poor, the dead,
Kneeling beneath two bleeding hands extended
  With Christ's dear blessing for each little head.

1865.

A NIGHT AND MORNING—1862-3.

O Memory, the fountains of thy Deep
   Are broken up, and all its fairy shells
Lie glimmering after each dim billow's sweep:
   Once we but saw the rose-bloom in their cells,
And melody was in the sounds alone;
We see the pallor now, and hear the moan.

Our images lie broken in the sand,
   Our blossoms wither'd in the mist, we say;
Our summer birds have left the snowy land,
   Phantoms of tropic songs, and flown away;
Our gorgeous buds have borne no golden fruit;
Our desert's singing springs are dry and mute.

Sweet souls have gone above the awful stars,
   Tired hearts are heavy in the dark below;
The world is blasted with the breath of wars,
   And Heaven folds close the Secret we would know;
Blind shapes of storm move in the gloom, and where
Is the white wing of Calm to light the air?

A NIGHT AND MORNING.

Weird Something, crown'd with bloody asphodels,
  In whose dark watch twelve moons dropp'd faded
    light,
We see thy red path mark'd with bursted shells,
  And ghosts of cannon-thunder haunt the night;
Thy sword has done its work, but work remains:
The victory waits for other ghastly plains.

Like Memnon, singing in old legend, we
  Have given to the setting light our sighs:
Great Angel of the Mystery to be!
  Help us to hail its unveil'd glory rise,
And lay the beauty of a faith divine,
The soul's myrrh-offering, on its morning shrine.

And if when its last sun is gone we moan
  Slow, tremulous dirges full of broken sound;
If whiter images are overthrown;
  If Time's most kingly hopes are yet uncrown'd;
If fiercer signs glare on the walls of Fate—
We know that God is God, and Man can wait.

ARMY OF OCCUPATION.

[AT ARLINGTON, VA., 1866.]

THE summer blew its little drifts of sound—
   Tangled with wet leaf-shadows and the light
Small breath of scatter'd morning buds—around
The yellow path through which our footsteps wound.
   Below, the Capitol rose, glittering, white,

There stretch'd a sleeping army. One by one,
   They took their places until thousands met;
No leader's stars flash'd on before, and none
Lean'd on his sword or stagger'd with his gun—
   I wonder if their feet have rested yet!

They saw the dust, they join'd the moving mass,
   They answer'd the fierce music's cry for blood,
Then straggled here and lay down in the grass:—
Wear flowers for such, shores whence their feet did pass;
   Sing tenderly, O river's haunted flood!

ARMY OF OCCUPATION.

They had been sick, and worn, and weary, when
   They stopp'd on this calm hill beneath the trees:
Yet if, in some red-clouded dawn, again
The country should be calling to her men,
   Shall the reveillé not remember these?

Around them underneath the mid-day skies
   The dreadful phantoms of the living walk,
And by low moons and darkness, with their cries—
The mothers, sisters, wives with faded eyes,
   Who call still names amid their broken talk.

And there is one who comes alone and stands
   At his dim fireless hearth—chill'd and oppress'd
By Something he has summon'd to his lands,
While the weird pallor of its many hands
   Points to his rusted sword in his own breast!

APRIL AT WASHINGTON.

O WHISPERING Phantom and fair
   Of the April of two years ago!
Rising here in the delicate air,
   How strange are the pictures you show!

I see you, with Triumph that sounds
   In the cannon and flashes in light,
Glide over these blossoming grounds
   Through the crowded rejoicing at night.

And I see you where steel is reversed
   To the funeral drum's stifled beats,
To the thought of a murder accursed,
   To the bugle's long wail down the streets;

To the dust, under bells moving slow
   With the weight of a people's great grief,
Among flags falling dark-draped and low,
   To the dead-march behind the lost chief:

APRIL AT WASHINGTON.

Who was wrapp'd in your beautiful hours
   As he pass'd to his glory and rest,
His coffin-lid sweet with your flowers
   And his last human look in your breast!

1867.

—— TO ——

Sweet World, if you will hear me now:
   I may not own a sounding Lyre
And wear my name upon my brow
   Like some great jewel full of fire.

But let me, singing, sit apart,
   In tender quiet with a few,
And keep my fame upon my heart,
   A little blush-rose wet with dew.